20 Ways To Implement Social Emotional Learning In Your Classroom

Easy-To-Follow Steps to Boost Class Morale & Academic Achievement.

KA'REN MINASIAN

ISBN 978-0692103609

TABLE OF CONTENTS

11. BUILD SMALL COMMUNITIES IN CLASS WITH STUDENT TEAMS

12. BUDDY UP WITH AN OLDER OR YOUNGER CLASS

13. GIVE INTERVIEW PROJECTS WHERE KIDS WRITE NEWS STORIES ABOUT THEIR CLASSMATES

Section 3: Personal Connections, Introspection, and Study

14. MAKE A PERSONAL CONNECTION WITH STUDENTS EVERYDAY

15. CREATE A PEACEFUL PLACE FOR UPSET AND ANGRY KIDS

16. HELP KIDS CREATE PERSONAL GOALS, & ADJUST THEM THROUGH THE YEAR

17. HAVE STUDENTS CREATE JOURNALS FOR FREE-WRITING & PROMPT WRITING

18. ASSIGN ART PROJECTS THAT INVOLVE EXPLORING THOUGHTS & FEELINGS

19. ASSIGN STUDENTS A JOB IN THE CLASSROOM TO TEACH RESPONSIBILITY

20. TEACH STUDENTS HOW TO MONITOR THEIR OWN PROGRESS

DEDICATION

I would like to dedicate this book to every teacher that continues to influence, mentor, and inspired students to be role models and leaders.

I cannot even begin to express how grateful I am for the teachers who came into my life exactly when they did. My respect goes out to all the men and women throughout the years with the passion and selflessness to share their wisdom, through books, talks, and seminars with those that are eager to learn and better not only themselves but those around them.

I did my best to absorb all that I heard, read, and experienced and honored to share my knowledge. The exercises, methods and suggestions in this book have been tried and tested over years of coaching and teaching others.

I am thankful for the opportunity to share the lessons that were passed on to me and I hope that in some way, I am able to serve you and the lives of those that you are impacting on the daily basis.

Ka'Ren Minasian
Kminasian@stormprogram.com
www.stormprogram.com

INTRODUCTION

THE IMPORTANCE OF SEL

Remember all the teachers you wanted to forget. The autocratic, "sit down and shut up" ones who made you feel dumb, afraid to raise your hand or ask them a question, who yelled at you for not having your homework, or having a scratchy handwriting, or failing your spelling test or getting most of your math problems wrong? They didn't respect us and we didn't respect them.

But then there was that special teacher, the one who changed your life and helped you grow into the person you are today. For me, it was my 6th grade Math teacher, an older man that always wore a tie and had wild hair. He had a calm voice and a kind smile and made me feel smart and talented.

The teachers we remember fondly tended to be kind, caring, understanding and made us feel special, smart and respected. In turn, we respected them. When we had a problem, they were the ones who took time to sit down with us and figure out why we having difficulty learning our multiplication tables or making sense of what we read.

They created **SOCIAL-EMOTIONAL LEARNING (SEL)** in the classroom before it had an official name.

The SEL classroom fosters open communication, understanding, kindness, polite communication and empathy and translates into respect for you, the teacher, and, among the students respect for each other.

The children in your class are focused and fully engaged and learn through inspiring and challenging content. They display self-confidence, and a community spirit that involves caring and respectful relationships with you and with their peers. All this translates into kids being capable of high-level academics.

For school is not just for learning the ABC's. It's every bit as important for students and teachers to learn how to get along with each other – to be kind and compassionate and empathic.

Why SEL?

Research has repeatedly shown that SEL is critical for success and well-being in life. People with social and emotional competence are more likely to:

- Have a sense of well-being in their personal lives;
- Act as contributors to their communities;
- Have meaningful relationships;
- Feel happiness in their work lives;
- Feel more optimistic about their future;
- Demonstrate compassion for others;
- And do better in academics as student performance improves when social and emotional development is fostered by instructors and institutions.

What exactly does an SEL approach teach?

SELF-AWARENESS

The ability to accurately recognize one's own emotions, thoughts, and values and how they influence behavior. The ability to accurately assess one's strengths and limitations, with a well-grounded sense of confidence, optimism, and a "growth mindset."

"self-awareness" skills:

- Identifying emotions
- Accurate self-perception
- Recognizing strengths
- Self-confidence
- Self-efficacy

Here are some examples to use in the classroom:

• At the beginning of the semester, have each student share a "one-minute autobiography" describing themselves and their life experience.

• Ask students about their previous experience with your subject, and solicit ideas about how they best learn.

• Begin class with a couple minutes of mindfulness to calm emotions and focus attention.

SELF-MANAGEMENT

The ability to successfully regulate one's emotions, thoughts, and behaviors in different situations — effectively managing stress, controlling impulses, and motivating oneself. The ability to set and work toward personal and academic goals.

"self-management" skills:

- Impulse control
- Stress management
- Self-discipline
- Self-motivation
- Goal setting
- Organizational skills

Here are some examples to use in the classroom:

- Include an academic planner as one of your required course materials. Provide a few minutes at the end of class for students to get started on their homework. Getting started is often the hardest part about getting it done.
- Use growth mindset oriented language when giving feedback to students (e.g. "you clearly worked really hard on that" instead of "you did a great job").

SOCIAL AWARENESS

The ability to take the perspective of and empathize with others, including those from diverse backgrounds and cultures. The ability to understand social and ethical norms for behavior and to recognize family, school, and community resources and supports.

"social awareness" skills:

- Perspective taking
- Empathy
- Appreciating diversity

- Respecting others

Here are some examples to use in the classroom:

- When studying characters (either fictional or historical), ask students to identify how the characters might have felt or be feeling.
- Acknowledge racism, sexism and other bias as it exists in your subject area and allow students to share their reactions.
- Get to know students' cultures and interests, using questionnaires or informal discussion, and integrate the curriculum with material that is relevant to their lives.

RELATIONSHIP SKILLS

The ability to establish and maintain healthy and rewarding relationships with diverse individuals and groups. The ability to communicate clearly, listen well, cooperate with others, resist inappropriate social pressure, negotiate conflict constructively, and seek and offer help when needed.

"relationship" skills:

- Communication
- Social engagement
- Relationship building
- Teamwork

Here are some examples to use in the classroom:

- Try to arrive a few minutes early to welcome students as they arrive, and stay a few minutes after class to follow up with students of concern.
- Be willing to engage with students if you see them outside of class.
- Get to know students' academic goals, ask them to reflect on how the class is connected to those goals.

RESPONSIBLE DECISION MAKING

The ability to make constructive choices about personal behavior and social interactions based on ethical standards, safety concerns, and social norms. The realistic evaluation of consequences of various actions, and a consideration of the well-being of oneself and others.

"responsible decision making" skills:

- Identifying problems
- Analyzing situations
- Solving problems
- Evaluating
- Reflecting
- Ethical responsibility

Here are some examples to use in the classroom:

- For subjects in which students look for solutions to problems, ask students to come up with multiple ways to find the solution. Facilitate discussion on the different approaches and ask students to identify and explain what worked best.
- Ask students to conduct self-assessments on their class performance, identifying strategies and behaviors that are

working well for them and anything that needs to be changed or improved. Self-assessment could be built in to the testing process, with a reflective assignment following return of exams and quizzes.

In this book you will learn how to:

- cultivate kindness in your classroom;
- connect with your class on a more impactful level;
- improve classroom engagement;
- equip your students to be more successful;
- create a positive, and creative environment.

SECTION 1:

SEL AS A CLASS

STEP 1

CULTIVATE KINDNESS in the CLASSROOM

"No act of kindness, no matter how small, is ever wasted."

~Aesop

Have you ever stewed because the old lady in front of you at the supermarket was taking too long to take her groceries out of the cart and put them on the conveyer belt? Ha! Why didn't you help her? Ask yourself that.

Kindness seems to be a lost gem these days, replaced by impatience and road rage.

Believe it or not, though we are hard wired to be considerate and kind. Year-old infants will pat the face of a crying infant, while toddlers will give their toy to a child sitting in time out. "The desire to help is innate," says David Schonfeld, MD, director of developmental and behavioral pediatrics at Cincinnati Children's Hospital Medical Center.

And a children's sense of doing good develops as they grow. Science shows that toddlers receive a rush of positive emotions when sharing, giving, and doing kind things for others. In fact, one study shows that 18-month-old children who sacrificed their own treat were happier than when they gave away a treat they had found.

Somewhere along the way, though we start to lose kindness and compassion for our fellow human beings. But we don't have to -- *if* we cultivate kindness in the classroom.

Acts of kindness cultivate shared happiness, build relationships, and give kids a sense of connectedness to a group, community, or place. Best of all, they are an excellent way to build a classroom community full of good will and optimism.

Getting Started

To cultivate kindness in your classroom, you first need to know these four basic principles:

First, rewards for kind behavior are unnecessary. Just the act of helping another child will release happiness chemicals that will make the child feel good. In fact, even viewing an act of kindness or courage elevates warm feelings in youth, and encourages them to do the same.

Second, altruism must start at the top of the school. Administrators and teachers must model kindness for students, and those acts of goodness will create a culture in which students do their part to show compassion through their inclination to create a school community ripe with good feelings.

Third, while kindness is natural for young students, they do need a push through reminders. As Albert Einstein once said, "A student is not a container you have to fill, but a torch you have to light up."

Fourth, you as their teacher need to show genuine gratitude for acts of kinds, which encourages kids to keep up the good work. Appreciation has proven to increase positive emotions and overall optimism among students, while creating satisfaction and a connectedness to their teachers, the school, and their life. It has also been shown to reduce emotional burnout among teachers.

Here are some ideas for cultivating kindness in the classroom:

- At the beginning of the year, read _Have You Filled a Bucket Today?_, a story about the power of kind words. Then create your own bucket for the classroom. Get a small tin bucket from a craft store and cut 3-by-3-inch pieces out of card stock. Kids can write messages of kindness, appreciation and love on the cards throughout the week to fill up the bucket. At the end of each week, spend a few minutes sharing these notes of encouragement to end the week on a positive note.
- At the beginning of the year, create classroom "Gratitude Books." Each week, a student brings the gratitude book home and the students and their families create a page

with pictures and descriptions of the things for which they are grateful.

- Have the students write "Gratitude Letters" for the school community and deliver to school employees, including school administration, food service staff, janitors, and maintenance.

- Have students write something that they are thankful for on a big piece of paper. Take photos of the students holding the paper. Frame the "Gratitude Pictures" and hang them in the classroom or the hall. Lastly, send them home as a gift to their family.

- Create a "Gratitude Bulletin Board" where students bring pictures to the class to explain, and then place on the board to create a class collage.

- Play "Gratitude Spies" in which students draw a student's name from a hat without revealing the name of the person they drew. During the course of the day, the students "spy" on their secret classmates, and at the end of the day, each student shares one or more things they are grateful for about the student. The obvious conclusion is that your kids will spend the day doing nice things to ensure they receive a good update from their spy.

- At the beginning of each Friday or Monday form a "Gratitude Circle" where students share an entry from their "Gratitude Journal." In the journal, students write about things they are thankful for, or they respond to a "Gratitude Quote." Only do this activity once a week otherwise research shows that it loses its impact.
- For the "Gratitude Quote," students will reflect upon their interpretation of a given quote.

To get you started, here are some quote ideas:

➢ "Feeling gratitude and not expressing it is like wrapping a present and not giving it." —William Arthur Ward

➢ "Let us rise up and be thankful, for if we didn't learn a lot today, at least we learned a little, and if we didn't learn a little, at least we didn't get sick, and if we got sick, at least we didn't die; so, let us all be thankful." —Buddha

➢ "Gratitude is one of the sweet shortcuts to finding peace of mind and happiness inside. No matter what is going on outside of us, there's always something we could be grateful for." —Barry Neil Kaufman

➢ "What you focus on expands, and when you focus on the goodness in your life, you create more of it. Opportunities, relationships, even money flowed my way when I learned to be grateful no matter what happened in my life." —Oprah Winfrey

• Hang posters that show helpful, healthy attitudes.

STEP 2

TEACH STUDENTS POSITIVE PHRASES to HELP THEM be RESILIENT through FAILURES

Every time eight-year old Samantha gets a C on her spelling test, she tears up the paper, flops on her desk and starts wailing. When ten-year old Billie gets only a B on his math test, he ends missing class the next day with his usual tummy ache.

On the one hand, we put lots of pressure on kids to succeed and on the other, as teachers and as parents we all want to protect kids from failing. But doing so is actually not good for them.

Not learning to tolerate failure leaves kids vulnerable to anxiety and to meltdowns when the inevitable failure does occur, whether it happens in preschool or college. And perhaps even more important, it can make kids give up trying—or trying new things.

What Kids Learn From Setbacks

Disappointments help kids learn to deal with setbacks. For one, it helps them develop characteristics they'll need to succeed, such as coping skills, emotional resilience, creative thinking, and the ability to collaborate.

And they learn to have what's called a "growth" mindset, vs. a "fixed" mindset.

Fixed Mindset

A fixed mindset fosters the notion that intelligence is something that you have or do not have, and does not evolve. When children think this way they refrain from taking on new challenges, and see effort as pointless because they don't have the "right stuff." And so, you know what happens. The child believes they have limited ability and gives up easily, thinking, "I'm dumb." "I can't do it." "It's too hard."

Growth Mindset

A growth mindset fosters the notion that intelligence evolves with effort and perseverance and all kids can become smarter In fact, the kids who produce the best work at school are not always the ones with the highest IQs; they are the ones with the most ambition and positive attitudes about themselves.

These students embrace challenges and look at effort as a journey. They don't give up and learn from criticism. They help their fellow students and find inspiration in their successes. They practice self-compassion and believe they are capable of success no matter the assignment or subject.

Your goal as their teacher is to make every child feel that he or she is capable of developing and becoming smarter and to make the class community an assembly of enterprising students who motivate one another.

Here's some ways to foster a growth mindset:

- Use positive phasing whenever possible. For example, telling kids they did a "GOOD JOB!" is the correct spirit.

But to foster a growth mindset even more, be specific, like "Your effort is really paying off because your writing has really improved."

- Have class discussions where you ask students what steps and strategies they took to find success on specific assignments, how they overcame obstacles, and what their performance taught them.

- Tell students that you appreciate their effort, and that is OK to take risks and fail sometimes on the way to learning.

- Create a poster as a class that illustrates the right and wrong ways to look at their worst moments in order to inspire hope for future improvement.

- Brainstorm with your kids to come up with better ways to move from a "fixed" to a "growth" mindset.

Here are some examples that you can use in your classroom.

Me and My Classmates say:

• "I like a challenge" instead of "I will stick with what I know."

• "How can we learn from one another" instead of "Everyone is smarter or better than me."

• "Let me try a different way" instead of "I give up."

• "How can I improve" instead of "I am no good at this."

• "Mistakes are part of learning" instead of "I failed."

• "My effort and attitude are everything" instead of "My abilities are everything."

• "Learning takes time" instead of "This is too hard."

STEP 3

CREATE ANCHOR CHARTS with YOUR STUDENTS

Anchor charts are a great classroom tool. They:

- Make thinking visible.
- Provide a way for students to highlight important classroom work and life notions.

- Help kids to recognize goals, understand concepts, set expectations, support instruction, as well as involve students in processes.
- Help students brainstorm ways to solve problems, which could be either general ideas or solutions to specific issues that you see in the classroom.

Teachers can use anchor charts for any subject, but they are incredibly useful for *Social-Emotional Learning.*

Topics that your class can use to make anchor charts include:

• "What does respect look like?" Student responses might include "Being helpful", "Playing fair", and "Listening to other people when they are talking".

• "Be a problem-solver not a part of the problem."

An example of an anchor chart from a teacher on Pinterest (which has a mystifying amount of chart ideas) attempts to solve the issue of what students should ask themselves before they turn in an assignment or test.

The teacher begins with the prompt:

"Before you say, 'I am through', ask yourself:"

Student responses might include:

• Did I do my best on the assignment?

• Did I include everything that the assignment required?

• Did I seek, listen to, and accept peer and teacher feedback?

• Is there anything I can improve?

• Am I satisfied that this is the best I can do?

The chart will look different depending on the grade level of your students.

STEP 4

ROLE-PLAY to DEVELOP EMPATHY

The best way to know what the other person is feeling is to walk in their shoes. And one of the best ways you can do this is to roleplay what wearing their shoes might feel like.

For children, role playing is a powerful way to help them practice an SEL skill like empathy.

Research tells us why: Social and emotional learning takes place in the brain's limbic system—the "feeling" mid-brain"-- which learns best with practice, one-on-one feedback, and positive motivation. Role-plays are a fun to build practice and to get one-on-one feedback into your SEL toolbox. And they help with motivation as well.

You can use role play to help children reflect on actions and develop knowledge to tackle any situation that might arise on the playground, in the classroom, or at home.

Students can wear costumes, make decisions in character, and expend some energy, while putting themselves in someone else's shoes.

The Teacher's Role

As the teacher, you are the director who explains the plot, so that everyone understands the scenario, and the students are the improvisational characters who use sentences that begin with "I" and state feelings, values, and beliefs to resolve the issue.

Give Everyone a Job

Assign the actors character names and make sure they understand their roles. Even if students are role-playing a situation that's based on real life, it's important that the real names of the participants not be used. This will help everyone focus on the problem being explored, not the people involved, which is a key component of conflict resolution.

Role-Play Basics

Have students call "Action" to begin the role-play. As you watch the role-play, keep the problem, the proposed solution, and the SEL learning targets in mind. Watch the actors' bodies closely and call "Freeze" at a moment of heightened physical expression. " And then the "audience" asks questions such as:

• What do you think will happen next?

• What could the characters do differently to find a solution faster?

• What are the characters feeling inside them right now?

Teachers can choose to restart the scene using insight from the audience or continue from the "freeze" point.

Choosing Roles

You can hand out cards to students, and give kids the opportunity to choose roles on their own, so they can put together a plan for the personality of their character.

Here are a few examples of what the role-playing card might say:

• "During recess, you notice that someone is all alone and looks sad."

• "During a partner work assignment, you are teamed up with someone who you feel does not work as hard as you."

• "During a test, you notice that someone is copying all of your answers." • "Your friends are teasing someone because they got braces."

• "You accidentally bump into someone, and they drop their lunch tray, and someone says you did it on purpose."

• "Someone tells a lie to you and your friends, and you know the real truth.

• "A classmate steals from another student, and they tell you they will harm you if you tell on them."

Helpful Tips

- Recreate the scene with different students, so that they can provide different reactions.

- Following the exercise, ask students who they thought handled the situation best, and who was the most admirable through their actions.

- After, ask them to synthesize each scene to underscore what approaches worked best.

STEP 5

REFLECT to CELEBRATE GOOD WORK & ADDRESS THINGS that NEED IMPROVEMENT

Have you ever experienced this? It's 2:35 and your class has just finished a science experiment. You realize there's only seven minutes to clean up from science and do everything else needed to do to walk out the door at 3:00 to go home. Suddenly there's all this flurry of movement, talking and chaos as twenty-five kids scurry in different direction to put things away, clean up and organize their desks.

Now imagine a different scenario. Let's say you organized your time so you ended the class at 2:20 and then sat the kids in a circle to reflect on the day—a daily reflective closing meeting.

Reflection Meetings

Students and teachers who hold reflection meetings enjoy a better classroom environment because it makes kids appreciate the idea of "community."

Teachers can do it once a week, or every morning to reinforce goals and set new ones while sharing "news" with one another, or at the end of the day.

As a class community, everyone talks about behavior expectations, social skills, accolades for students who are always awesome and those who are improving, and a discussion of those things "the class" can do better to make a more productive and respectful climate.

Like a city council meeting, there are established meeting rules, and the class addresses them before each gathering.

Rules include:

• Have fun in a respectful way.

• Make room for everyone's ideas.

• Look at your friends when they are talking, preferably in the eyes.

• If it is not your turn to talk, it is your turn to listen.

• Listen, so that things move smoothly and quickly.

The meeting then moves to greetings that include eye contact, while using names and proper handshakes.

A quick activity is done by the students, which can be something involving "gratitude."

Then, the current class leader presents the news of the week or day.

Students can present the news with or without a "nudge." A nudge could be a "question card," which provides a prompt for the student leader who is providing "the news.

News questions cards read something like the following:

• Tell us what you did last summer.

- Tell us what you are going to do this weekend.

- Tell us about your favorite food, or sport, movie, game, song, television show, book, activity, etc.

- Share a funny story.

- Share your favorite memory.

- Share the most interesting thing about yourself. Tell us about your last dream.

- Tell us something that you have learned, and something you would like to learn.

More Tips

Read a poem or a passage from a book and reflect on how it made students feel.

Congratulate students for the things they are doing well, provide ideas for how they can improve, and go over the class's ongoing goals, which might include:

• We will treat everyone with kindness.

• We will worry about ourselves.

• We will quietly and quickly transition from one activity to the next.

• We will raise our hands to speak and listen intently to others.

• We can have our polite opinions, but will not argue with other students or the teacher.

SECTION 2

SEL in TEAMS, PARTNERSHIPS,

and GROUPS

STEP 6

"STRATEGIC" & STUDENT-CHOICE PARTNER ASSIGNMENTS

In Mary Johnston's 3rd grade classroom, the first step in a student's writing assignment isn't to scribble away but a conversation with a peer. Students explain their ideas to a partner, respond to questions, and push each other to more fully explore their thoughts before they put them down on paper.

Working with partners is a powerful way to promote SEL in the classroom.

Partnerships:

- Help students develop their cooperative learning skills while building a class community.
- Assist students with learning how to manage themselves in varying organizational frameworks

- Show students how partnerships can be useful for getting more work done in a shorter timeframe through cooperation and organization. This helps the social and personal development of each student.

How to Implement Partner Learning

- Allow kids to make their own partner choices, but also use strategy to partner students, so that they learn how to manage different types of relationships with students of varying personalities.

Here are the possibilities:

• Random selection through a blind draw, so there is perceived "fairness" and to show the random rules of the world.

• Teacher selection to ensure balance between "talkative students" and quiet ones, a boy with a girl, and other "diverse" equations, so students can learn from one another.

• Self-selection. This is a good choice on occasion to see how well partnerships form in your class. But it has drawbacks because high-achievers tend to couple up, girls and boys stick to their own gender, and children sometimes get left out, which could harm self-esteem.

- Work with student teams to massage any issues they have during the process.

Here are some issues:

  o Younger students do not understand the benefits of teamwork right away, and individual students in a two-person team either tend to do all of the work, very little work, or argue about how they should share the work, because they do not know how to effectively collaborate. In the end, however, the ideas of their peers stimulate new ways for students to approach assignments, and the children learn the varying abilities of other students they may have never thought were possible because of stereotypes and prejudice.

o Students at any age tend to pigeonhole their peers when they do not share commonalities. Nevertheless, much can be learned when two students with different personalities or backgrounds work together to solve a problem, which in the long run reduces the instinct for children to immediately stereotype people based on appearance, ethnicity, culture, or personality.

At the beginning of the class, explain the meaning of "stereotypes" and prejudice, and that it is irresponsible to judge others before learning to know them and work with them in a meaningful way. Give them a class assignment about stereotypes and prejudice before working on a team assignment. In the appendix, we have provided a lesson plan with the objective of helping students understand how unfair judgments of individuals and groups, and how stereotypes and bias negatively influence our lives.

- Explicitly explain the "speaker" and "listener" role once students are paired. Hand out a picture of a mouth and an ear, and inform the student with the mouth that they can express their ideas, while the students with the ear must listen. After a few minutes, the students exchange the picture, and follow the same rules.

- Emphasize that it is just as important to be a "good listener" as it is to be a "good speaker."

- Explain that good partners do the following:

  • Talk to each other

  • Listen to each other

  • Compliment each other and show gratitude for one another

  • Ask respectful questions of one another.

- Use the Think-pair-share technique. It works well in team assignments, as it models how to work in a collaborative way within a partnership.

It works in this way:

- Students analyze an issue on their own.

- Students share their analysis with a partner.

- Students share their analysis with the class. This helps students to see how an individual's analysis differs from their own, how they feel about their partner's analysis without the guidance of a larger group, and how the larger group reacts to both their analysis of an issue and their partner's. The result should be a collection of information that shares individual views as a part of an overall worldview. For example, show your students the cover of a book and have students write down what they believe will happen in the book. Students then read to their partners what they think will occur, and then they share their ideas with the class.

- Do a "think-pair-share" following the same strategy, except on the second time through, the paired students must synthesize both of their ideas into one collective thought, and share it with the class, which teaches collaboration and negotiation.

STEP 7

GROUP ASSIGNMENTS to FOSTER NEGOTIATION & LEADERSHIP SKILLS

We all know that leaders are those with alpha genes, whether male or female, and not every kid is going to be president of his or her class. Does that mean beta kids cannot develop leadership skills? Absolutely not.

Through group assignments, every student can learn how to better negotiate with each other and to develop leadership skills that will help them succeed better in life. It's all about teaching kids to work "AS" a group not "IN" a group through co-operative learning.

Co-operative learning is beneficial in the following ways:

• Raises the achievement of all the students.

• Builds positive relationships where children learn to value diversity.

• Provides experiences required for social, emotional, psychological, and cognitive development .

Teachers Role

- Determine ideal group sizes with the understanding that the bigger the group, the more interactions between students, and the greater the challenge for everyone involved, including the teacher.
- Roam the room and help the groups, and each member of the group to stay focused and engaged and remain respectful of each other's opinions, regardless of the many kinks they will encounter and must endure.
- Support the students learning, and delegate group tasks.

Set Up Groups

Here's how.

- Consider that a "pair" requires two interactions, a triad group requires six interactions, and a quad group requires 12 interactions.

- Work your way from pairs to a group of four. In this way the students can evolve through each possibility as the number of interactions grow, which ultimately provides enrichment through a range of contributions.

- When students work in a triad for the first time in your class, you should do a similar activity to the one you did in pairs. This time there will be **listener**, a **speaker,** and an **"encourager,"** who makes sure that the listener and speaker are working together, taking turns, and speaking clearly.

Assigning Key Roles

When students move to groups of four or more, the teacher should assign key roles to each member of the group, or the teacher can allow the group to assign roles to one another.

A good starting point to use, or adapt, is Bennet and Dunne's key roles:

• **The manager** keeps the group on task, guides the activity, and makes sure that everyone contributes and has a voice.

• **The encourager** promotes tolerance and encourages everyone to voice his or her thoughts and contribute through praise and gratitude.

• **The spokesperson** reports activity information to the teacher and the class.

• **The record keeper** takes notes, summarizes and clarifies all ideas, and shares them with the group. If children are too young to keep notes or a person is not a good speller then encourage them to take risks with their writing or keep "mental notes".

• **The secretary** is responsible for gathering and distributing resources that the group needs.

• **The evaluator** tracks the progress and makes notes regarding what students contribute to the group and how well everyone works together. Then, they create an evaluation at the end of the activity, and reflect on the group's success. Before doing a major activity and assigning key roles, use the "jigsaw technique" to get your students comfortable with working in a group.

Here is how it works:

1) Divide the learning material into four segments. For our example, let us use the structure of the earth, so the four segments would be crust, mantle, outer core, and inner core.

2) Divide the class into quad groups, and give each child a number from one to four.

3) Each student studies his or her assigned Earth layer.

4) The students now form "expert groups", which means that all of the number "ones" form a group (of at least four students), the number "twos" form a group, etc.

5) The expert groups discuss what they learned with one another and come up with the main points concerning their Earth layer.

6) The kids then return to their main group and share what they learned from their meeting with the expert group members.

This strategy for introducing kids to groups is easy to monitor, and is useful to teaching your students the diverse way their classmates think in a structured and investigative way while also teaching the difference between "cooperation" and "competition."

STEP 8

Use PEER MEDIATION to TEACH PROBLEM SOLVING & CONFLICT MANAGEMENT

When I taught younger grades, one of the banes of my existence was the constant complaining, "He pulled my pigtails." "She balled up my paper." "He pushed me." On and on. Yes of course, kids should turn to the teacher to help solve conflicts and to trust the teacher to make a swift decision between right and wrong. But often issues come up that they could solve on their own, if they had the skills and did not feel compelled to immediately go to a teacher whenever conflict occurs.

Let's face it. Life demands independence and, at some point, children will have to learn how to solve problems and resolve conflicts on their own. Why not start in the classroom where, as every teacher knows, there is no shortage of conflicting stories and ongoing battles between students.

Peer Mediation

Peer mediation is a process where same age students resolve disputes together or in small groups with the teacher's help.

The idea behind peer mediation is to,

- empower students to be peacemakers;
- learn how to regulate their behavior through self-monitoring;
- judge what is appropriate through situational analysis and the offering of differing perspectives.

Ultimately, children learn to resolve situations through negotiation and mediation, which translates into greater empathy and making better choices.

Integrating Peer Mediation into the Classroom

Here are the steps for integrating peer mediation into your classroom.

Step One--Negotiation. Teach all students the power of negotiating constructive resolutions to their conflicts through these four phases.

One: Have students define the conflict.

Two: Have students exchange perspectives on the matter.

Three: Have students negotiate options for mutual gain.

Four: Students reach a peaceful, smart decision.

Step Two--Mediation: Mediation in a classroom can be done by:

- **Teachers**
- **Class ambassadors**--children who have exhibited pragmatic leadership skills. Teachers can train them to assist kids with negotiating conflicts through modeling, exercises, and role-playing activities.
- **Older kids** –Training students from an upper grade level instead of using students from the same grade has some

advantages, because younger students are more likely to respect the older students, and the older students are less likely to show favoritism.

The "Peacemaker" presents the following guidelines:

• **First,** the mediator explains, "Peer mediation is voluntary. I am neutral, and therefore, I will not choose between right or wrong. Each of you will state your views on the situation, and my role is to help you find a solution to your conflict that both of you agree is acceptable."

• **Second,** students must agree not to interrupt one another and not to resort to name-calling, be honest and keep the matter confidential, solve the problem, and follow through on the agreed-upon solution.

• **Third**, if the students cannot agree on a solution between the two of them, the teacher will mediate the conflict.

In general, it is important to go through the following ideals with your class, so they understand how to deal with any conflict they might have with a classmate:

• Respect the right of everyone to disagree with you.

• Open up yourself to differing points of view.

• Listen carefully and ask questions before you rush to judgment.

• Be patient and understanding.

• Imagine more than on solution to every problem.

• Be willing to compromise.

• Negotiate mutually fair agreements.

STEP 9

ALLOW STUDENTS STRUCTURED & UNSTRUCTURED TIME for TALKING with THEIR PEERS

Let kids talk during class? This seems counterintuitive to class management and impulse control. But its effectiveness in reducing problems in the classroom might surprise you. In fact, structured and unstructured talk time helps kids build confidence, understanding, and social skills.

When to Implement Structured and Unstructured Talk

The best time for a chit chat is when your students are squirming in their seats, and it becomes contagious. Give the kids a break and let them have five minutes or so of engagement among themselves, then refocus and reengage them. If you don't hit the reset button during these times, your students stop learning.

If you are uncomfortable with letting your students have five minutes of unstructured, talk time about the topic at hand, then have a structured-talk time activity planned when the kids lose focus. This happens quite often near the end of the school year or before long break and holidays.

Here is one talk-time activity that you can pull out when needed. It works well to expend a little energy, as well as a way for students to team build and get to know their classmates.

Detective

In the game "Detective," students receive a worksheet with ten questions about the topic.

- Students pair up, ask each other one question from the worksheet, and write down the answer.
- After both students have asked and answered one question, they find another partner and ask each other the next two questions.

- The students continue the process until each question has an answer.

- Once the students are back at their desks, they discuss the answers either with their already-established desk group or through formed groups. The children work together until there are no discrepancies in any of the answers.

STEP 10

PLAY GAMES that PROMOTE COOPERATIVE LEARNING

We all want our kids to learn how to work with one another, to become critical thinkers, and apply these skills to accomplish team goals. One of the best ways to accomplish these goals and for the kids to have FUN in the process is through team-building games.

Team-building games take the edge off textbooks and tests, and they provide a reprieve to the day's core activities by teaching cooperation and communication. Together, both support collaborative critical thinking, and are valuable to creating a positive classroom climate.

Team-Building Basics

Kids love to imagine a life of intrigue, so offer them a scenario requiring teamwork to survive or negotiate, whether it is a shipwreck, a zombie apocalypse, or an adventure to find a lost treasure. For example, students must figure out a way to survive on a deserted island before coming up with a solution to finding their way back home.

Students come up with their own ideas, share them with their team, and through group consensus, they must plan their best escape to find safety.

Cup Stack Game

A kinetic option to team-building is the Cup Stack game, which challenges a group of students to build a pyramid out of six cups. The pyramid consists of three cups at the bottom, two in the middle, and one on top. The catch is that students cannot touch the cups with their hands or any other part of their body!

Here is how it works:

• Students tie strings to a rubber band, according to the number of students in the group.

• Each student holds on to his or her end of the string.

• The kids collectively attempt to pick up a cup with the strings and rubber band, and build a pyramid one cup at a time.

• After the activity, the teacher asks students questions regarding how members of the team accomplished their goal. For clarity, the following image of the "Cup Stack" teambuilding game comes from "Ms. Sepp's Counselor Corner":

Questions the teacher can ask the students after the activity:

• Why was teamwork important to accomplish the goal?

• What did you learn about yourselves and your teammates?

• What skills did you need in order to be a team player?

• How can you apply the teamwork lesson in the classroom and outside of the classroom?

STEP 11

BUILD SMALL COMMUNITIES in CLASS with STUDENT TEAMS

An amazing way for students to learn to get along is to teach team spirit and a sense of belonging. To do so, create student communities in the classroom in which kids create their own "countries" complete with rules, motto, and flag. They will also create a map of their country with a name, and names for the capital and major cities. Collaboration and "democratic processes" are the keys to developing the ideals of the country:

Here are some other questions that students can answer about their country:

• Are their beaches, jungles, farmland, forests, or urban cities? Describe them in detail.

• What types of vegetation and animals exist in the country?

• What is the climate?

- What is the history of the country?

Describe the folklore or mythology surrounding the people who inhabit the country.

- What goods does the country produce, and what is the country's major industry?
- What does the country export and import?

By creating communities with a culture, the students within the group work harder in groups and as individuals because of community pride.

STEP 12

BUDDY UP With AN OLDER OR YOUNGER CLASS

A great way to quickly build relationships between students and staff is to create Buddy Classrooms. These are classrooms from different grade levels that meet routinely to create bonds between older students as models and younger students. Kids are always amazed at how easy it is to find common ground with younger or older students. The big kids feel important and the little kids feel special.

There are many powerful ways these classroom connections can become even more powerful for your school.

Here is some.

1) Reading Buddies -- younger students can read to older students and vice versa, create book commercials together, book chats, and more.

2) Art Projects -- create art projects together, with the older buddy partner doing the more intricate processes.

3) Science Experiment Teammates -- create a science experiment that buddies can do by collecting data, building, and then experimenting and sharing the findings.

5) Sharing Good News -- When a student does something to celebrate, they go to their buddy room and receive praise, a cheer, or even earn time with the buddy classroom.

7) Technology Projects – Having an older buddy introduce younger students to technology makes it easier for the younger student to learn new software or hardware.

8) Writing Stories -- Students can write a story together with the older student help the younger one to develop their story and with proper grammar.

STEP 13

Create INTERVIEW PROJECTS where KIDS WRITE NEWS STORIES about THEIR CLASSMATES

An important part of the SEL curriculum is encouraging understanding diversity and having empathy for all people. To further this goal, assign interview projects in which kids interview their classmates, and write a magazine article or blog on a student. Once they write a news story about the other and they learn the background and experiences of their classmate, they understand the other better and gain a new perspective.

This can be done several times a year, especially when you notice conflict between students.

Remember, this is "work." In other words, a formal interview is much different from a casual conversation between two people, and the teacher will have to explain this to their students.

Questioning their Peers

Students will need to come up with their own set of questions, and you must teach them how to ask questions that go beyond a "yes" or "no" answer.

Here are some options to nudge them along:

• Where and when were you born?

• Describe your family's history.

• What are you favorite subjects?

• What type of food does your family like?

• What activities do you enjoy?

• Where does your family go when they take trips?

• What scares you?

• What makes you happy?

• What do you want to do before you graduate high school?

• What do you want do after you graduate college?

Section 3: Personal Connections, Introspection, and Study

Step 14

MAKE a PERSONAL CONNECTION with

STUDENTS EVERYDAY

Start every day by personally connecting with each one of your students to let them know they have your back. This is a simple thing to do to ensure that students feel secure as the day begins, to positively define their mood as they start the day, and to set the tone for the day.

Here's how:

- Make eye contact with each of your students in the morning before school begins.

- Greet them by name and a simple greeting – "Good morning Jackson."

- Pay them a compliment – "That red jacket is really cool."

- Let them know you are happy they came to at school, even if their hair is too long or their skirt is too short, or they are not prepared with a pencil, notepad, or their homework assignment.

- Ask them how they're doing in a nurturing way. This is a great opportunity for a student to share personal information about things that happened outside of school that makes them feel anxious or depressed. In this way, you will understand if something happened to account for distressing behavior and you won't feel the need to reprimand them for forgetting their homework, or send them immediately to the office if they shoved the child next to them. Understanding will replace punishment that would only add to their distressed state and further wreck the day for learning, as well as possibly causing damage to your relationship with the student and their relationship with the school.

- To further your own empathy, imagine how much better a student, who has had a rough night or morning, might feel if greeted with you reaching out and touching their hurting heart versus meeting them with a reprimand or harsh words.

- Be consistent and authentic--that depressed child with a troubled home at least has your smiling face to begin the day. They at least have the security of your classroom where they can be vulnerable and feel loved.

The chart on the next page explains some creative ways to welcome your students, but do not try anything that feels awkward to you because your kids will sense it immediately.

Visit the appendix for a chart that can help you and your kids express their emotions as they enter the classroom.

Step 15

CREATE a PEACEFUL PLACE for UPSET and ANGY KIDS

We all know how maddening it is when something at work riles us and, with nowhere to run, we just sit and stew and find it hard to focus on our work. Students feel the same when something upsetting happens in the classroom and, unable to let off steam they end up either withdrawing or act outing. Neither helps them learn, while acting out typically throws the whole classroom into a tizzy.

The way to get around this disruption is to make a quintessential part of your classroom a "peaceful corner"-- a place for kids to work out their emotions on their own, without your direct intervention or punishment.

Such a "peaceful place" allows kids to:

- Identify which emotions lead them to their inappropriate behavior;

- Identify alternative ways to conduct themselves next time they are confronted with the same situation;

- Manage their emotions in order to calm down.

Teacher's Guide

Before students begin using your class's peaceful place, explain its objective through a class activity, in which you explain strategies for calming down, so that students can refocus and get back to learning.

During the activity, talk to kids about what types of emotions cause them to lose focus, including anxiety, anger, or fear.

Discuss what types of feelings students must have to stay engaged with learning objectives, including focus, curiosity, calmness, quiet, satisfaction, and joy.

The Peaceful Place

Explain to your class that their peaceful place is a corner of the room in which students go when they are upset or angry and cannot focus.

Explain that is NOT a time-out or punishment, but a place to assess their emotions and find focus before returning to the class or their group.

Tell them they can draw, write, read, do a puzzle, or listen to calming music to help them soothe emotions and visualize calm and satisfaction.

Finally, explain the guidelines for entering the peaceful place. These might include the following:

- The peaceful place is for anyone who is feeling angry, worried, upset, or just needs a five-minute break to refocus.
- A voluntary signal is used by the student or a suggestion by the teacher to go to the peaceful place to gather their emotions.
- Only one person at a time may use the peaceful place.

- There is a time limit of five minutes, which can be counted using a sand timer.

Designing a Peaceful Place

Provide the following:

- A few pillows or a beanbag chair.
- A box with a few small puzzles.
- A book or two.
- Some drawing paper and map pencils.
- A journal where kids can write out their feelings as well as how to solve them, and read the entries of other students.
- A stuffed animal and a stress ball.
- "Calming strategy cards." *Liz's Early Learning Spot* offers a set of 23 calming cards for free.

Step 16

HELP KIDS CREATE PERSONAL GOALS, & ADJUST THEM THROUGH THE YEAR

As a teacher, you want all your students to succeed in life. To help them do this, it's important to teach them how to set goals and ACHIEVE them—starting at a young age. This will help them learn to set appropriate benchmarks and teach them:

Responsibility: Success or failure depends on what they put into it.

Time management: Kids learn how to manage their time to meet their goals.

Self Confidence: Nothing beats the feeling of meeting your own goal.

Resilience: Kids learn to cope with the small setbacks that might stand in their way.

Perseverance: They learn to keep trying and rework their steps until they meet their goals.

Here are ways to help them set their goals:

- **Confront unrealistic goals.** Sometimes kids choose goals so big or so out of their element that it's nearly impossible to meet them. Encourage them to choose goals that are realistic.

- **Choose just-out-of-reach goals.** Teach kids to try and to choose goals that are attainable but also just out of reach. In doing so, they learn to push themselves to meet a new challenge versus hiding out in the comfort zone. Explain that if they don't meet a goal in the time allotted but only get very close there's value in trying.

- **Set specific goals.** Kids love to generalize when it comes to setting goals. For instance, they might say things like, "I want to be the best reader in the class." But what does that mean? How can that be measured? Encourage them to shoot for a more specific goal, like "I want to be able to read and then correctly retell the story of Charlotte's Web."

- **Break it down.** Teach kids to break down their goals into smaller, manageable steps.

- **Set checkpoints.** Have the kids create a poster board to map out their goals. On the top of the poster, they write the main goal for the year. Underneath, they write the steps they can take along the way to reach the goal. With a visual aid in place, they can check in on their goals monthly (or weekly) and check off steps as they accomplish them.

- **Establish a Bucket List**. Have your kids create a bucket list of all the things they want to do in their lifetime. Then, students will share their lists with the class, and refine it to five things they want to do the most.

- **Set Short and Long-term goals.** Have kids write out goals they would like to do that day, that week, that month and perhaps even that term, depending on the grade level.

- **Assist them.** Once students have established their ambitions, work with them so that they understand what they need to do to accomplish their goals. This should tie back to their immediate goals in the classroom. Work with your students on an individual basis to create goals for the grading period, the year, as well as life goals, and explain to them how they all interplay.

- **Revisit and Revisit.** Allow kids to revisit their goals and revise them if they wish. You never want to hold a child to the goals they created while young.

Step 17

Have STUDENTS CREATE JOURNALS for FREE-WRITING & PROMPT

Journaling is a great activity for kids. This is especially so for those who are reluctant to speak or write, as it is a non-threatening and practical means for students to explore ideas about themselves and other topics and to express their feelings without an audience.

Here are the benefits of daily writing in a journal:

- To enable kids to confidently write, and improve, without the red pen that fills them with dread.

- To allow for repetition of writing patterns, grammar and punctuation practice, and introspection, all of which helps the child permanently solidify a concept in their brains.

- To enable teachers to assess their student's writing to see how they are developing, and to figure out what they need to teach or re-teach.

- To provide valuable insight for better class management of problem areas, and better relationships with students who might need emotional assistance, a little more one-on-one time during difficult periods in their life, and assistance with problem-solving.

- To allow kids who can only draw and label their drawings with simple words to identifying their weak areas and strengths, as they grow their ability to write longer phrases.

Helping Them Write in a Journal

Introduce a specific skill, and ask them to use it while writing before you set them off on a free-writing exercise.

Sometimes free-writing is difficult, so a nudge, not necessarily a prompt, might be needed to get some students rolling. Have a list somewhere visible to help kids get started. The ideas are simple beginnings to stories, like the following:

- "Something happened to me."

- "I went to a new place."

- "I have a pet."

- "I have a favorite treat."

- "I have a favorite game."

- "Someone upset me."

- "Something made me happy."

- "What if I had three wishes?"

Reserve official prompts for deeper thought exercises, but do not forget to make it fun, too. Here are a few examples of writing prompts that go deep as your students stretch their social-emotional learning:

- You really want your friend to spend the night with you, but your parents won't let you because you have school the next day. Use your journal to convince your parents that they should allow your friend to stay with you for the night.

- The school has decided to raise money for a charity. Who do you think deserves the money? Explain the reasons why your choice is the best one for the donation.

- Your school has decided that it will only teach two of the following three subjects: music, gym, and art. Which two subjects should the school keep? Explain why you think those subjects are more important than the other one.

Visit the appendix for an example of more writing prompts.

Step 18

Assign ART PROJECTS that INVOLVE an EXPLORATION of THOUGHTS & FEELINGS

Students often feel emotions that are impossible to put into words. Artistic expression can work out those issues like no other activity.

Art projects provide an outlet for young children to explore their emotions, and even gain control of them. Research also shows that art fosters cognitive abilities as well by triggering the imagination. This stimulates and expands your students' minds to think on a new level, and to be more inventive and flexible with their notions.

The following are more reasons why art should be included in your curriculum for social and emotional growth, and cognitive evolution:

- If children practice creativity, it will come natural to them as they get older, which opens up the mind for innovative ideas.
- Children who are exposed to art at least three days a week are four times more likely to become academic high achievers. They are also more confident and outgoing.
- Art strengthens critical-thinking skills as children learn how to express themselves and their emotions through creativity.
- Art helps develop fine motor skills in young children, as well as visual-spatial skills.
- Art is challenging, so children learn perseverance and focus, which is required for introspective creativity.

Self-portrait

Self-portraits are one of the better ways for kids to reflect upon how they feel about themselves and their life. They are very revealing at times, and offer a cathartic way to work out negative emotions and express positive vibes about themselves.

Here's how to get them going.

- Use Picasso-style drawings for an art study of one's self. Begin with a brief lesson on Pablo Picasso and cubism, which could be a video or a short biography.

- Play a round of "Roll a Picasso" so the students have an idea how to create one of their own "Picasso's" before moving onto a self-portrait.

- Have students roll a die four times to find out what style of facial feature they must use, and then they draw and color their creations. There is no need for perfection, or even erasing, because there are no mistakes when putting together a Picasso.

- Have the class show their "Roll a Picasso" artwork and compare their work to some of Picasso's originals.

- After your students have a clear understanding of how the cubism formula works, it is time for the students to create portraits of themselves.

- Let them know that there is no wrong way for the kids to interpret cubism or themselves, so release them to reflect and create. Each student will make a head shape and then attach eyes, noses, and mouths with cutouts, in any way they please.

Step 19

Assign STUDENTS a JOB in the CLASSROOM

to TEACH RESPONSIBILITY

Class jobs teach responsibility and give kids ownership of the shared class. When they do their job well, they feel proud and this enhances self-esteem.

Student Jobs

A student's first job is to keep their desk area organized and clean, and their belongings in one place. Next, all students need to assist with an overall orderly and organized classroom.

Teacher Assigned Jobs

Teachers come up with a list of jobs that require no supervision. To keep things fair in the eyes of the students, assign jobs randomly and rotate the tasks each grading period. For fun, have students fill out a job application or even create a resume, so they understand the process of finding a job.

Here are some ideas for classroom jobs:

- **Attendance Taker**: Checks the roll every morning, and counts students who are absent or tardy.
- **Lunch Count Helper**: Tallies students who are buying lunch.
- **Mail Carrier**: Goes to the office each day to collect the teacher's mail from their box.
- **Pledge Starter**: Stands in front of the class and leads the Pledge of Allegiance.
- **Homework Collector**: Collects homework at the beginning of the day and puts it in the teacher's basket.

- **Paper Passer**: Passes out worksheets and resources to students.

- **Paper Collector**: Collects worksheets and resources from students.

- **Media Assistant**: Helps the teacher when he or she is using any media that might include an overhead projector, laptop, or tablet.

- **Centers Monitor**: Ensures that centers are organized and proper materials are available.

- **Chair Stacker**: Stacks classroom chairs each day for easy vacuuming in the evening.

- **Janitor**: Makes sure there that the floor is clean of debris after projects and at the end of the day.

- **Horticulturist**: Waters and maintains the classroom plants.

- **Lights Monitor**: Makes sure the lights are off when the class leaves the classroom, and the lights are on when the class enters the classroom.

- **Door Monitor**: Opens and closes the door when the class enters or leaves the classroom.

- **Errand Runner**: Runs errands for the teacher.

- **Teacher's Assistant**: Helps the teacher with anything they need like stapling papers and making copies.

- **Class Manager**: Monitors the class job board and reminds students when they forget to do their job, and fills in when a student is absent from the class.

Once you have assigned jobs to your students, display them in your classroom. A good way to keep track of each person's task is to create a chart with jobs and use a clothesline pin to attach a student's name to that particular job. That way your class can use the chart more than once when students receive new jobs.

END the DAY through REFLECTION

As previously noted, it's a great idea to end the day with reflection. This will help you to determine what stuck with your students at the end of the day, how students are feeling, what went well during the day, and what they found difficult.

It is important that you do not send any student home feeling lost or confused. They need to know that you care about their progress and that you cannot wait to see them the next day. That way, regardless of what goes on at home that evening, they know that they have you as a sanctuary each morning when they arrive to class.

Using a sticky note, have students write their feeling about the day and place it on the "ticket out the door" chart before leaving the classroom.

Students can use the "ticket" to answer a specific question that you pose, or to provide a general feel for how things went during the class day.

Conclusion

I hope you that you enjoyed this book and will use it as a resource on your campus. It will not only positively improve your students' classroom experience, but impact your life as well in unexpected and even profound ways.

Commit to teaching SEL today to create a better, kinder, and more compassionate world of tomorrow.

Thank you for your continued commitment to our children and education. I am proud to be your partner and are looking forward to impacting future generations.

Ka'Ren Minasian

www.stormprogram.com

APPENDIX

CREATE an SEL LIBRARY & USE STORY TIME for

TEACHABLE MOMENTS

Here are five stories to get your class started right away for
SEL story time and teachable moments, provided by Free
Stories for Kids. When you present the story to the class, you
want your kids to answer the following questions:

• What is the character trait associated with the main
character?

• How do you know that is the character trait?

• Why is the character trait important?

• In what ways do you connect to the character trait?

Story of Will: August Heat

August Heat was a little city mouse who lived peacefully in a big house. The house had all the comforts any mouse could ever dream of; there was always warm water to bathe in, hot food, plenty of clothes and whatever else.

A rather unusual kind of mouse lived with August. His name was Percy Veering, and despite all those comforts, every day he would give something up. He could quite easily wash in cold water as if it were warm, or chew leeks as though they were lumps of cheese. The worst was when he tried to convince August that acting in this way would be for his own good.

"Come on, man, you'll make yourself stronger. You're becoming a real softy!" Percy would say to him.

And poor August would turn away, snuggle into his blanket, and read a good book, wondering how there could be such stupid people around.

Misfortune would have it that, one night, so much snow fell on the city that our two friends' little mouse-house was completely snowed in and cut off from the outside world. They tried to get out, but the cold was intense, and they didn't think they could dig a tunnel through so much snow. They decided to wait it out.

The days went by, and still the snow remained; now there was no food left. Percy endured it quite well, but August - deprived of his hot baths, his food, and his warm shelter, was on the verge of losing control. He was a cultured kind of a mouse, who had studied widely; he knew that he wouldn't be able to stand more than three days without food. This was the same amount of time they had worked out they would need to dig a tunnel through the snow. They now had no choice but to get digging.

But as soon as he touched that cold snow, August turned away. He couldn't do it. Not with something so terribly cold, not even as hungry as he was, not even knowing that he would soon die!

Percy, though, managed it quite well, and started digging, all the time encouraging his friend to do the same. But August was paralyzed; he just could not stand such terrible conditions. He couldn't even think straight. Then he looked at Percy, 'that idiot', and understood that that mouse was a lot wiser than he looked. Unlike himself, Percy had trained himself to do things because he really wanted to do them, and not just because they were the most appealing things to do at any given moment.

He could order his legs to dig regardless of whether they were purple with cold - something which was impossible for August, no matter how much he wanted to do it. And with those thoughts, and a tear of helplessness, he lay down upon the mountain of feathers that was his bed, ready to let himself die.

When he opened his eyes, he thought he was in heaven; the face of an angel was smiling at him. But then with great joy he realized that it was just a nurse. She told him they had been treating him for days, ever since a very brave mouse had arrived at the hospital, his four legs frozen, and given instructions on where to find August. Then the brave mouse had passed out.

When August ran to thank Percy for all his help, he found him standing up, having greatly recovered. Percy had lost several fingers, and an ear, but he looked cheerful enough. August felt very guilty since he hadn't lost a thing.

Percy told him, "Don't worry, if it hadn't been for those fingers and that ear, I wouldn't be here either. What better use could they have had?!"

Of course, they continued to be great friends, but August no longer thought of Percy as an idiot. By Percy's side he set about regaining control over his own pampered and demanding little body, each day giving up one of those unnecessary comforts of modern mouse life.

Story of Fortitude: The Warm Whale

Gail the Whale lived in a small salty lake. She was the only whale in that territory, and she led a very comfortable life. In fact, this easy life made her a bit fussy. But, one year, there was such an incredibly hot summer that the lake's water really warmed up. Gail, used to such an ideal existence, could hardly stand the hot water. A little fish, which had spent some time in a child's goldfish bowl, told Gail that humans used fans to cool themselves down in summer. From then on, Gail the Whale couldn't think of anything else apart from how to build her very own fan.

Everyone told her that she was overreacting, and that the hot weather would soon pass, but Gail got to work, constructing her enormous fan. When it was finally finished, she started fanning away at herself.

Unlucky for the fish!

The giant fan beat the little lake's waters so strongly that huge waves rolled right across it. The waves crashed onto the lakeshore, leaving the lake half empty, and Gail stranded in only a few inches of water.

"You couldn't just hang on for while. You had to empty the lake," some unhappy-looking fish berated her.

"So impatient! So selfish!" others shouted.

But the worst of it for Gail was not the insults, but the fact that with so little water around her, the heat was becoming unbearable. Preparing herself to die of heatstroke, she said her goodbyes to all her friends, and they asked for her forgiveness. She assured them all that if she were to live again she would be stronger and learn to put up with life's discomforts.

Yet, once again, Gail the Whale was overreacting. She managed to survive those hot days without dying, although, of course, she suffered. When the next rains arrived, the lake filled up again, and the weather improved. Naturally, Gail had to keep her promise, and show everyone that she had learned not to be so dependent on comfort, so impatient, and so fussy.

Story of Forgiveness: A Frog and the Frying Pan

Fran the Frog was the best chef in the whole swamp, and all the toads and frogs of the region enjoyed coming to her very select restaurant. Her 'Flies in spicy bug sauce' and her 'Caramelized dragon flies wings with honey of bee' were the kind of delicacies that every self-respecting frog should try; and that made Fran feel truly proud.

One day, Toby came to her restaurant, ready for a nosh. Toby was a great big toad, and certainly wasn't the brightest. When Fran's fine creations were brought before him he complained, saying that that wasn't food, and that what he really wanted was a botfly burger. Fran came out of the kitchen to see what the problem was, and Toby told her that these dishes weren't good enough for - and certainly wouldn't fill - a Smooth Newt. This made Fran so offended, and furious, that she went to the kitchen, came back with a frying pan, and whacked Toby squarely on the forehead.

A slight scuffle ensued.

Even though Fran realized she should have controlled her temper, and she kept asking Toby to forgive her, the toad was so angry that he said he could only forgive her if she handed him the frying pan so he could hit her back. Everyone tried to calm Toby down, knowing full well that, given his strength, he could easily crack little Fran's head open with that frying pan.

Toby would not accept an apology, and Fran felt awful for having bashed him, so she tried everything. She gave him a special cream for bruises, she poured him an exquisite puddle water liqueur. Even better than that, she cooked him a... beautiful botfly burger!

But Toby the Toad still insisted he would not be satisfied until he got to return the blow he had received. It had reached the stage where he was almost getting out of control.

Then a very old toad entered the restaurant, shuffling along with the help of two crutches.

"Wait, Toby," said the old toad -you can give her a whack after I've broken your leg. Remember that you are the reason why I have to walk with these crutches.

Toby didn't know what to say.

He recognized the old toad. It was Reddit, his old teacher. When Toby was small, Reddit had saved him from a bunch of young hooligans. In the process, Reddit had lost a leg. Toby remembered that it had all happened because he had been highly disobedient, but he had never given a thought to Reddit until now...

Toby now realized he was being very unfair to Fran. Everyone, including himself, made mistakes sometimes. And if we are to return blow for blow, wound for wound, all we are doing is prolonging the damage. So, even though his head still hurt and he thought Fran had made quite a remarkable mistake with that frying pan, seeing her feeling so sorry, and doing everything she could to put things right, Toby decided to forgive her.

Apology accepted, they spent the rest of the evening laughing at what had happened, and enjoying wonderful botfly burgers. And everyone heartily agreed that that was a rather better idea than getting into problems with pans.

Story of Commitment: The Leopard in His Tree

There was once a leopard in the jungle; and a very nocturnal leopard he was too. He could hardly sleep at night and, lying on a branch of his magnificent tree, he spent his time watching what was happening in the forest at night. This is how he came to learn that there was a thief in that forest. He would watch the thief go out every night with empty hands and return loaded up with his stolen loot. Sometimes the thief had nabbed the senior monkey's bananas, other times he had filched the lion's wig, or pinched the zebra's stripes. One night he even snuck home with the big elephant's false tusk, which the elephant had been secretly wearing for quite some time.

However, as the leopard was a very quiet sort of cat, who lived at the margin of everything, he didn't want to say anything to anyone. He didn't see it as his business, and, if truth were told, he rather enjoyed discovering these little secrets.

And so, thanks to the stealthy thief, quite a stir was being created in the world of the animals: the elephant felt ridiculous without his false tusk, and the zebra now looked like a white donkey, not to mention the lion who, now as bald as a lioness had lost all respect. Most of the other animals were in some similar position too. They were furious, confused or ridiculous, but the leopard lay quietly in his tree, each night enjoying the thief's escapades.

However, one night the thief went on vacation, and after having waited a long while for him to appear, the leopard grew tired and decided to sleep for a while. When he woke up he found himself in a place very different from his usual tree, he was floating on the water of a small lake inside a cave, and around him he could see all those objects which, night after night, he had seen being stolen... the thief had cut down his tree and stolen his entire home along with the leopard himself!

Well this was the last straw, so the leopard, taking advantage of the thief not being there, ran out and went straight to see the other animals to tell them where the thief had hidden all their things...

They all praised the leopard for having discovered the thief and his hideout, and allowing them to recover their possessions. In the end, the animal who lost most from all this was the leopard, who couldn't replant his magnificent tree and had to make do with a much inferior tree located in a very boring site... and he regretted having not been concerned at the problems of the other animals, now seeing that in the long run those very problems had become his own.

Story of Effort: The Wailing Forest

There was once a forest made up of tiny trees that were all growing up together. They had been planted by a very old laborer who took care that they would all grow up to be straight and healthy. However, the area was battered by strong winds, and the little trees preferred to avoid the bothersome gusts, so they bent their trunks and branches to shelter themselves.

The old man, knowing they could never grow well like this, set about straightening them out, and spent many hours tying their slim trunks to supporting posts, hoping his beloved trees would understand he was doing this for their own good.

But those naughty trees had no desire to put up with all that wind. It mattered not to them that the old man would promise them that when they were tall and upright the air wouldn't bother them a jot. They always got by by bending and twisting themselves, hiding from the wind. Only one of those trees, one located right in the middle of the forest, forced itself to grow up straight, patiently bearing the annoying gusts.

The years passed, and the old man died. And from then on the trees could grow however they liked, bending and crouching from the wind just as they pleased, with no one bothering them about it. All, that is, except the single straight tree in the center of the forest, who remained determined to grow up just as a tree should.

But as the forest grew, and the trees got thicker and stronger, they began to hear cracks from inside. Their branches and trunks needed to keep growing, but the trees were so twisted that the inexorable growth they were experiencing only brought them pain and suffering, even more than the suffering they had avoided by staying out of the wind. Each day and night, in the depths of the forest, one could hear the cracking and snapping of the trees, and it sounded like groans and sobbing. And around that area the place became known as the wailing forest.

And it was a place with a special charm since, right in its center, surrounded by thousands of short, knotty, twisted trees, rose one impressive tree that was long and straight like no other. And that tree, the only one that never creaked or cracked, continued growing and growing, without a worry for the capricious wind and its accomplice, the breeze.

"STRATEGIC" & STUDENT-CHOICE PARTNER ASSIGNMENTS

The following is a lesson plan with the objective of helping students understand how unfair judgments of individuals and groups, as well as stereotypes and bias, negatively influence our lives, before beginning partner assignments.

1) Begin the lesson by discussing with your students how people use labels or categories to describe others based on characteristics like clothing, looks, or the groups in which they belongs. Explain that categorizing is a natural human behavior, but it is irresponsible to make assumptions about people that they do not know.

2) As a class, brainstorm labels that people use at school to categorize people like "nerd", "jock", etc. On the board, write each category, and then have students narrow the list down to five major categories.

3) On separate pieces of flip chart paper, write the five categories down and hang them in the room. Allow your students 10 minutes to travel to each category and write down other adjectives related to the stereotype. For younger students, the teacher might need to do this part of the lesson as a class as well.

4) When the students are finished, ask them to take a moment and look at the adjectives that the class has generated under each group heading. Use the following questions to lead a discussion about what they recorded:

5) Do assumptions apply to everyone in a group?

6) Do most people hold the same assumptions about a group? Why or why not?

7) Do assumptions tell us anything definite about an individual?

8) How do assumptions affect your behavior towards people?

9) Now, ask students to help define the word "stereotype." Explain that when we make assumptions about an entire group of people, those assumptions are referred to as stereotypes. When assumptions and stereotypes influence our attitudes, we may find that making a fair judgment about someone or something is difficult. This influence on judgment is called a "bias."

10) Take another look at the adjectives recorded and hold a class discussion around the following questions: Do these adjectives describe a stereotype? How can they be unfair or hurtful?

11) Explain to your students that the same thing happens to people of varying cultures and races.

12) Ask students to spend 15-20 minutes writing or drawing, depending on age, about a personal experience with biased behavior.

13) Prompt the class with the following questions before they begin:

• How did you know that you were being unfairly judged?

• What words or actions were directed at you because of assumptions or stereotypes?

• Why do you think those assumptions were made about you?

• How did the experience make you feel?

• How do you think you should have been treated in that situation?

14) When students are finished, have them share their experiences with the class if they are comfortable doing so.

Made in the USA
Columbia, SC
06 June 2021